Praying the Right Way

By

Chris Oyakhilome

BELIEVERS' LOVEWORLD INC.
a.k.a Christ Embassy

UNITED KINGDOM:
Christ Embassy International Office
363 Springfield Road
Chelmsford
Essex, CM2 6AW
Tel: +44 1245 490 234

SOUTH AFRICA:
303 Pretoria Avenue
Cnr. Harley and Hendrik Vewoerd,
Randburg, Gauteng,
South Africa.
Tel: +27-72-241 7332

NIGERIA:
Christ Embassy
P.O. Box 13563, Ikeja,
Lagos, Nigeria.
Tel: +234-802 3324 188,
+234-805 2464 131,
+234-1-892 5724

email: cec@christembassy.org
website: www.christembassy.org

Contents

INTRODUCTION

I once read an interesting story about Charles Grandison Finney. It was said that he had been attending a church meeting for some time and wouldn't give his heart to Christ. He wouldn't so much as say a word of prayer during the times of prayer.

While he was in one of those meetings, somebody asked him, "Why don't you pray, Charles?"

"I'm not going to pray because I've been attending this meeting for so long, and from what I can see, it doesn't seem like you folks get any answers," he retorted.

Later on when he was born again and filled with the Holy Ghost, he found out why those folks didn't get any answers to their prayers – they were praying the wrong way!

Finney made this observation almost a century ago, but it's sad that many in the Body of Christ are still in the same dilemma today. Many Holy Ghost-filled, tongue-talking, Bible-quoting believers live frustrated lives simply because they're not receiving answers to their prayers. Some will confide in you that they don't really know what to pray for and how.

To many of such people, prayer is just a part of their religion. They believe they have to pray because God requires them to, but they don't even know why they pray. They pray, neither knowing what to say nor whether to expect answers; but God's plan is to answer our prayers.

However, there are myriads of questions on this all-important subject of prayer that arise in the minds of many. It would seem that there are as many questions on the subject as there are people.

"Why are my prayers going unanswered when Brother So-and-so always seems to receive everything he asks God for?"

"How do I pray in different situations and under different circumstances?"

"What about the Lord's Prayer?"

"Why do I have to pray, anyway? God knows my needs, and He can meet them without my praying, can't He?"

Some even ask the most fundamental question: "WHAT IS PRAYER?"

God's Word, however, is very clear on the subject and teaches us all that we need to know to pray right and get results. The problem with the many who pray and get no answers to their prayers is that they pray wrongly because of their ignorance of what the Word says about prayer.

There's a right way to pray, and one of the privileges of having the Holy Ghost is that He becomes our Teacher Who shows us from God's Word how to do things right.

Through the years, the Holy Spirit has guided me to teach several times on the subject of prayer, and some of the wealth of information and revelation released through those teachings have formed the basis for this book. I encourage you to open up your mind and your heart as you read, and allow God's Word and His Spirit to instruct you, correct you and teach you how to pray the right way.

CHAPTER ONE

THE RIGHT PERSPECTIVE ON PRAYER

A lot of people wonder why their prayers are not being answered and things aren't working right for them. Well, that's why prayer is such an important subject, and we must know the right way to do it.

The first thought that must be established in your mind for you to be able to pray effectively is this: *God wants to hear and answer your prayers. If He had planned it any other way, He would never have required you to pray.* That's why He said,

> If my people, which are called by my name, shall humble themselves, and pray, and seek my face, and turn from their wicked ways; then will I hear from heaven, and will forgive their sin, and will heal their land (2 Chronicles 7:14).

Consider the Lord Jesus: He always received answers to His prayers. He never once prayed in vain. When we pray we should not expect to have any less than He. That's because He's given us the authority to use His name. When we speak in His name, it's as authoritative and effective as Jesus Himself speaking to the Father.

Sadly, though, too many Christians don't know this because they don't spend enough time studying the Word. So they don't enjoy a personal relationship with God.

We need to know God as our Father and our Friend; One Who's not far away and Who can be trusted. If God is a stranger to you, then you can't trust Him; that's the reason for doubt. But when you know Him, you'll have faith in Him, and when you have faith in Him, you'll trust Him.

GOD IS MORE WILLING TO GIVE TO YOU THAN YOU'RE WILLING TO RECEIVE

> And it came to pass, when he was in a certain city, behold a man full of leprosy: who seeing Jesus fell on his face, and besought him, saying, Lord, if thou wilt, thou canst make me clean (Luke 5:12).

Notice this man didn't question the power of God. He knew God had the power to heal him. As a leper he had heard about Jesus the Healer, so he wasn't questioning His power to heal him of his leprosy. His only problem was he didn't know if Jesus would be willing to heal him. In other words, he knew Jesus *could,* but he didn't know if He *would.*

There are a lot of people like this: They know God can, but they're not sure He wants to. They don't know His will. They're the ones who say, "Well, I don't know if it's God's will to heal me," so they run to the doctor for help. If it's not God's will to heal you, and you go to the doctor to get healed, you'll be committing a sin by trying to get something (healing, in this case) that's not God's will for you to have!

A lot of times, when it comes to spiritual things, we're quick to say we don't know God's will, while at the same time, we demonstrate a desire for good things.

Philippians 2:13 says, *"For it is God which worketh in you both to will and to do of his good pleasure."* That desire for good things is a reflection of God's desire in us. There's no father who wants his children to go through the same problems he went through. If you're a good parent, you won't plan for your children to have the kind of trouble you had. You work hard so they won't have to suffer.

You couldn't be better than God in taking care of your family. If you're more willing to do good things for your family than He, then He's not qualified to be Who we call Him. But if God is God, and He is Who His Word says He is, then He's better than the best daddy on earth. God is more willing to provide for you than you could ever be willing to receive provision. He desires to bless you and give you good things more than you're ready to receive them. That's why

Our Father *loves us and wants the Best for us* ♡

Jesus said you don't need to make vain repetitions when you pray. It doesn't matter what your need is, you must get this idea and let it affect your prayer life.

That leprous man knew Jesus was the Healer and that He could heal him, but he wasn't sure if He wanted to. This is the reason many don't receive miracles in their lives today. They're not certain that God is willing to do something for them. It's the same reason some even believe God put a sickness on them to make them humble and keep them from some other problem.

God doesn't need the devil's equipment to train His children! Why would He use Satan's tools as instruments of righteousness after He told us he's a murderer and the father of lies? If God could put sickness on you to humble you and you took drugs to take away God's instrument for your required humility, that invariably means you and Satan are in the same camp, lying against God!

But we're the generation that's not questioning the will of God, for we've come to accept God as our Father.

That leper said, "Lord, if thou wilt, thou canst make me clean." No one had been willing to touch him because of his terrible disease, but Jesus touched him to show him how willing He was to heal him. The Bible says, "And he (Jesus) put forth his hand, and touched him, saying, I will: be thou clean. And immediately the leprosy departed from him" (Luke 5:13). That statement: "I will: be thou clean" settled for all time and in all generations any questions or doubts about God's willingness to heal.

I Will: Be thou clean

EXPECT ANSWERS WHEN YOU PRAY

Some people don't bother praying because even when they do, they don't expect answers. If you don't have a relationship with God through Jesus Christ, that is, you're not born again, you shouldn't expect answers because He wouldn't even hear you. However, if you're God's child, you have a right to expect answers when you pray. But to have those answers consistently, you must pray according to God's Word revealed in the New Testament concerning prayer.

God invites us to pray; He's not troubled with our prayers. Some people think they shouldn't bother God with their prayers because He already has a lot of problems to solve. They figure that with so many people calling on God at the same time, He might just get confused, and so in order not to compound His problems, they decide not to pray to Him. Don't think that way about God. He's not confused by our prayers. Don't wonder how He hears when so many people pray to Him at the same time. Remember, He is God! Nothing is impossible with Him.

When you pray, God listens because you're His child, and you pray according to His will. While listening to you, He doesn't consider your prayer with respect to another person's. He doesn't hold something back from you just because another person has asked for the same thing you asked for. He relates with you on a personal level.

God doesn't prefer one of His kids above another; He relates with you as though you're the only one in the whole wide world. Did it ever occur to you that if you were the only person on earth, Jesus still would have come to die for you? That should let you know just how personal God is with you. He said, "Ask, and ye shall receive, that your joy may be full" (John 16:24). This is God's Word to you: If you ask Him, you shall receive!

People get a lot of encouragement to pray, but a lot of times they don't know how. It's one thing to tell people to pray and to pray hard, but it's another thing to let them know how to pray in such a way that they can have the desired results and make the necessary impact.

GOD MAY HAVE SAID IT, BUT YOU CAN STILL CHANGE IT!

Through prayers, we can prevail in circumstances. God has shown us in His Word that we can change anything, including things that were divinely destined to be. This may sound incredible to you, but it's in the Bible. God may have said you're going to have it one way, but if you discover you don't want it that way, you can change it. It's amazing, but it's true. The only times something can happen to you as God said it would are when:

    I.   You want it to happen.

   II.   You don't know it's going to happen.

  III.   You know it's going to happen, but you don't know what to do to change it.

IV. You don't do what you should do, even though you know it's going to happen.

God doesn't run our lives the way we think He does. Whenever He wants to do something nobody can change, nobody gets to know about it until it's done. Moses said the things that are revealed belong to us and to our children, but the things that are not revealed belong to God (Deuteronomy 29:29). So when He doesn't want any human influence on it, and when there can be no human influence on it, He doesn't reveal it! But if He reveals it to you, He is telling you if you want to change it, you can. And you can only change it when you pray, and pray the right way!

Key

There are several accounts in the Scriptures of men who changed the mind of God from what He had determined to do. One such account is in Exodus 32:7-14, where we read of how Moses stood between God and the children of Israel. God had determined to destroy them for their rebellion and stubbornness and raise a new generation from Moses, but Moses prevailed on God and prevented Him from doing as He had purposed.

Another instance is in 2 Kings 20, where one man changed the course of an event that had been divinely ordered of God. King Hezekiah had been sick to the point of death, and one day, the prophet Isaiah walked into his room and declared, "Thus saith the Lord, Set thine house in order; for thou shalt die, and not live" (2 Kings 20:1).

This was undoubtedly the Word and mind of God concerning Hezekiah's situation. He was doomed to die by none other than God Himself, and there seemed to be no way out. But the next verse states, "he turned his face to the wall, and prayed unto the Lord" (2 Kings 20:2).

King Hezekiah pleaded his case with God, and the Bible says:

He turned his face to the wall and prayed unto the Lord!

> And it came to pass, afore Isaiah was gone out into the middle court, that the word of the Lord came to him, saying, Turn again, and tell Hezekiah the captain of my people, Thus saith the Lord, the God of David thy father, I have heard thy prayer, I have seen thy tears: behold, I will heal thee: on the third day thou shalt go up unto the house of the Lord. And I will add unto thy days fifteen years; and I will deliver thee and this city out of the hand of the king of Assyria; and I will defend this city for mine own sake, and for my servant David's sake. And Isaiah said, Take a lump of figs. And they took and laid it on the boil, and he recovered (2 Kings 20:4-7).

Talk about changing a hopeless situation!

We can plead with God to change something

18

CHAPTER TWO

UNDERSTANDING PRAYER IN THE NEW TESTAMENT

For the New Testament believer, prayer is not just a means of religious communication with God; *it's a fellowship.* Some people pray because they've been brought up to think it's a religious obligation they must fulfill. True, the Lord Jesus said, "Men ought always to pray and not to faint" (Luke 18:1), letting us know prayer is a spiritual obligation for every believer. But that's not all that God intended prayer to be.

Beyond that, we need to understand the subject of prayer – the things to pray about and how to pray about them.

Prayer is more than merely talking to God. Many people pray, and yet many don't, but among the many who pray, a lot don't have answers to their prayers because they pray without understanding.

We need to understand that when we pray, we're making contact with the divine essence within us. This contact strengthens our relationship with God. Prayer is one sure way of getting yourself focused on God and getting a "rub-off" in His presence.

Prayer also has its place in bringing God's Word to pass in our lives. There are certain things we see provided for us in God's Word, but we need to do more than merely confess to possess them. Someone may say, "I'm full of the spirit of wisdom and revelation," but it doesn't come just by confessing it, otherwise Paul wouldn't have prayed for the Ephesian church that God would grant them the spirit of wisdom and revelation in the knowledge of Him (Ephesians 1:17). You've got to pray for that Word to take root in your life.

YOU CAN CHANGE ANYTHING THROUGH PRAYER!

Remember, the Lord Jesus said in Luke 18:1 that we should pray always and not give up. Through prayers, we can change things. We can change the course of our lives and our circumstances. We can change things in our homes, our jobs, our finances, and our bodies. We can even change things in the lives of other people, things in our schools, our cities, our nation and the world! This is why it's so important that we study and understand how to pray effectively. In Matthew 17:20, Jesus said,

> verily I say unto you, If ye have faith as a grain
> of mustard seed, ye shall say unto this mountain,

20

Wheat

Remove hence to yonder place; and it shall remove; and nothing shall be impossible unto you.

Jacob and Kashayla ♡ going to church

I like it when Jesus talks like this. It gives me the reason to be hopeful and believe that anything, absolutely anything, is possible! A man had brought his lunatic son to Jesus' disciples to cast the devil out of him. His disciples tried and couldn't, so he took his boy to Jesus, Who then cast the devil out of the boy.

The disciples later asked the Master why they couldn't cast the devil out, and He answered them, "*because of your unbelief.*" Then He added, "If ye have faith as a grain of mustard seed, ye shall say unto this mountain, Remove hence to yonder place; and it shall remove; and nothing shall be impossible unto you" (Matthew 17:20).

Now, a grain of mustard seed is so small that if you put several of them in your palm and blow just lightly, they'll fall off. Jesus said if you have faith as small as that grain of mustard seed you will say to a mountain to move from here to there, and it will! Then He said, "NOTHING SHALL BE IMPOSSIBLE UNTO YOU!"

If He had said nothing shall be impossible unto God, it would have been easy enough to agree with; everybody ought to know that. But He said nothing shall be impossible unto YOU.

Jesus also said in Mark 9:23, "All things are possible to him that believeth." So the big question is: Do you believe, and what do you believe? If you believe God's Word and put it to work in your prayer life, then anything is possible!

Put it to work in my prayer life.

DO I Believe God WORD

21

DON'T JUST SAY PRAYERS, PRAY FROM YOUR HEART!

At many family altars, family members come together to *say* their prayers, but in this dispensation of the Church where we've been born again and filled with the Holy Ghost, we don't *say* our prayers, we pray!

God's Word doesn't teach us to say our prayers but commands us to pray. There's a difference between praying and saying prayers. A lot of people have prayer books from which they recite prayers every day. They even recite the Lord's Prayer (we'll take a closer look at this in chapter 4) from their prayer books. It is important that prayer is heartfelt, even if you're reading or reciting it.

God hasn't called us into religion; Christianity is not one of the religions of the world. Christianity is the pulsating life of the resurrected Christ in the spirit, soul and body of a human. It's the divine life of God imparted to a human spirit here on earth. It's God's life at work in a man. The Christian doesn't look for God because he has already found Him. He doesn't try to reach God because he's already met Him, and he's not trying to appease God because he's already at peace with Him.

JESUS IS NOT MEDIATING BETWEEN US AND GOD

The book of Hebrews lets us know that Jesus is our great High Priest before the Father (Hebrews 2:17; 3:1; 4:14; 8:1;

9:11). He is also our Advocate (1 John 2:1). His ministry as our great High Priest and advocate, however, doesn't include praying to the Father for us.

I've heard a lot of people say Jesus Christ stands in the gap between the Father and us, but what the Bible teaches is that Christ Jesus is the Mediator between God and men, not between God and the Church. So He stands between God and sinners, not between God and His Church.

In 1 Timothy 2:5-6, Paul says, "For there is one God, and one mediator between God and men, the man Christ Jesus; who gave himself a ransom for all, to be testified in due time." This is talking about the whole world and God, and someone standing in the gap. Jesus is man's Kinsman-redeemer, Mediator and Umpire. But for us who have been born again, He's not our mediator because we don't need a mediator anymore.

True, Jesus is our Redeemer because He redeemed us and saved us, but since He brought us in and made us to sit with Him at the right hand of the Father, we don't need Him to mediate between us and the Father anymore. We've been brought to live right in the Father's presence. This is why it would be wrong and ineffective for us to pray to the Father *through* Jesus Christ our Lord. This is explained further in the next chapter.

CHAPTER THREE

PRAYING IN THE NAME OF JESUS

B efore you were born again, the Name of Jesus was given to you so you could come through that name to God and be saved. Jesus said, "I am the way, the truth, and the life: no man cometh unto the Father, but by me" (John 14:6).

In other words, He said, "Come to God through Me!" Now you've accepted His invitation and have come to God through Him. Having come to God and received eternal life and the divine nature, you became one with Him. You became a citizen of the kingdom of God.

Now that you're in His kingdom, you have His kind of life, you have already come to the Father, and you don't go back. You came to the Father once through Christ, and having come to Him, you don't keep going and coming; you stay in His presence! This is why you cannot and should not pray *through* Jesus Christ our Lord.

You may have prayed this way for a long time, but that doesn't make it right. You may even say it worked for you. It probably didn't, and you thought it did, but even if it worked, you were a baby then, and God overlooked your ignorance. Now it's time to grow up!

What is revealed from God's Word in the New Testament is praying to the Father *in* the Name of Jesus. Some folks don't understand this, and that's why they have problems getting answers to their prayers. They've had so many of their prayers go unanswered that they've lost all confidence in praying.

As long as you keep praying to Jesus or through Jesus, or you keep asking Him for things, your prayers will remain unanswered.

There's a great difference between praying through Jesus and praying in His name. To pray through Jesus is to pray through a medium to God, and that's unacceptable because that makes Him a medium, and He is no medium to the Christian.

However, when you pray to the Father in the Name of Jesus, you're exercising the power of attorney He gave you to use His name. This means you're operating the full legal powers He gave you to act in His stead and on His behalf. When you pray in His name, it's as though Jesus Himself were speaking, and everything responds to you the same way it would to Jesus.

IN HIS NAME

A New Day, a New People and a New Way to Pray

Jesus said in John 16:23, "And in that day ye shall ask me nothing." This means, "You shall not pray through Me or to Me." I know there are some Bible translations that render this verse as, "You shall not ask Me any questions," but that falls short because it doesn't fit within the context. They had been asking Jesus a lot of questions before this point, and that's probably the reason those translators thought He meant they should ask Him no more questions. But when you read further, you'll discover He wasn't talking about questions, He was talking about prayer.

> And in that day ye shall ask me nothing. Verily, verily, I say unto you, whatsoever ye shall ask the Father in my name, he will give it you (John 16:23).

Here the Lord Jesus lets us know there's a new kind of prayer for a new kind of people, the New Testament people. And He tells us, "You'll not have to pray to Me because whatever you ask the Father in My name, He will give it to you." So in this new day, what we do is pray to the Father in Jesus' name. Notice He didn't say, "You shall pray to the Father through Me." He said, "You shall pray to the Father in My name." The next time you hear somebody pray "through Jesus Christ our Lord, Amen," just know that prayer didn't have an answer because it didn't work!

Pray to the Father in Jesus name!

27

PRAY To the Father

We don't ask Jesus for anything in the New Testament, but we can tell Him how much we love Him; we can worship Him, praise Him and give Him thanks, although we also give thanks to the Father in the Name of Jesus Christ. We pray to the Father in the Name of Jesus and not to the Lord Jesus Himself.

A lot of times people pray without thinking about or listening to what they're saying. For example, they say, "Dear Lord Jesus, I pray in Jesus' name." That's ridiculous. How can you pray to Jesus in the Name of Jesus?

In the New Testament, we don't pray to Jesus in Jesus' name, we pray to the Father in Jesus' name.

The New International Version of John 16:23 says, "In that day you will no longer ask me anything." Another version puts it this way: *"you will not pray to me."* Here, the Lord Jesus wasn't talking about a particular twenty-four-hour day He had appointed after He got to heaven, nor was He talking about the day of crucifixion. He was referring to the day of salvation, the day of the new creation, the day in which the righteous shall enter into the gates of the Lord. That's the day we live in today.

THE POWER OF ATTORNEY TO USE THE NAME

Hitherto have ye asked nothing in my name: ask, and ye shall receive, that your joy may be full. These things have I spoken unto you in proverbs: but the time cometh, when I shall no more speak unto you in proverbs, but I shall shew you plainly

In the name of Jesus!

of the Father. At <u>that day ye shall ask in my name</u> (John 16:24-26).

Back then, in the Old Testament, the people couldn't ask anything in the Name of Jesus because the time hadn't come to do so. But then He told them that when the time came, they would have to ask the Father in His name.

There are folks who teach that when we pray, Jesus takes our prayers to the Father and starts begging Him to do something about them. Then the Father, after a lot of begging and cajoling, eventually says, "All right, all right, Son, because of You, I'll do it!" No way! Jesus expressly said He wouldn't do that; it's right there in the Bible!

> At that day ye shall ask in my name: and I say not unto you, that I will pray the Father for you (John 16:26).

Did you see that? He's telling us He doesn't have to talk to the Father on our behalf, and He lets us know why – "<u>the Father himself loveth you.</u>" The Father loves you Himself; He doesn't need anybody talking to Him on your behalf. That's why Jesus isn't praying to the Father on your behalf. Instead He says, "Don't come through Me, go by yourself, because the Father loves you. All you need is to use My name because My name is in charge of the New Testament."

In the New Testament, we have the power of attorney to use the Name of Jesus. He gave us the legal right to stand in

His stead and act on His behalf. This is too much for the religious mind to comprehend, but it's the truth all the same. This is the reason we can command a cancer to die in the Name of Jesus, and it dies. It's because He gave us the power of attorney to act for Him!

[handwritten: command something in the name of Jesus!]

"In That Day"

When Jesus went into the holiest place in the presence of the Father to present His blood as the sacrifice for sin, He went there as our representative. From the moment we believed in His redemptive work and accepted Him as our Lord and Savior, we were brought into the presence of the Father within the veil. Now, we don't go in and out of His presence. That's our dwelling place, and that's where we'll remain forever.

Where Jesus said, "In that day you shall ask Me nothing," He meant, in other words, "You shall not pray to Me for anything." He also said, "Whatever you ask the Father in My name, He will give to you." Notice He didn't say, "Whatever you ask the Father in My name, He will give to you if you believe and have faith in Me."

Jesus talked so much about faith that if He didn't include it here, it couldn't have been an oversight or error of any kind. He had said before, "If ye have faith as a grain of mustard seed, ye shall say unto this mountain, Remove hence to yonder place; and it shall remove; and nothing shall be impossible unto you" (Matthew 17:20).

"If ye have faith, and doubt not, ye shall not only do this which is done to the fig tree, but also if ye shall say unto this mountain, Be thou removed, and be thou cast into the sea; it shall be done" (Matthew 21:21).

"Be not afraid, only believe" (Mark 5:36).

"If thou canst believe, all things are possible to him that believeth" (Mark 9:23).

"Have faith in God" (Mark 11:22).

This time, however, He purposely didn't include the faith element. All He said was, "In that day, you shall not pray to Me but whatsoever you ask the Father in My name, He will give to you."

This is because "in that day," which is "this day," only those who are born again, who are called the believing ones and who have faith in the ability of Jesus' name are privileged to ask the Father in His name. They don't need to believe because they're already the believing ones. They don't need to be told to have faith because they're already the children of faith!

JESUS – NAME ABOVE ALL NAMES

Wherefore God also hath highly exalted him, and given him a name which is above every name: that at the name of Jesus every knee should bow, of things in heaven, and things in earth, and things under the earth; and that every tongue

should confess that Jesus Christ is Lord, to the
glory of God the Father (Philippians 2:9-11).

The Lord Jesus wasn't given a name that's recognized in
heaven only. His name has influence in heaven, earth, hell, and
the grave. Jesus has been given a name that is greater than every
name. The statement: "at the name of Jesus every knee should
bow, of things in heaven, and things in earth, and things under
the earth; And that every tongue should confess that Jesus
Christ is Lord, to the glory of God the Father" is not a promise
but a sovereign declaration of Almighty God. It's a law!

> And whatsoever ye shall ask in my name, that
> will I do, that the Father may be glorified in the
> Son. If ye shall ask any thing in my name, I will
> do it (John 14:13-14).

> And in that day ye shall ask me nothing. Verily,
> verily, I say unto you, Whatsoever ye shall ask
> the Father in my name, he will give it you.
> Hitherto have ye asked nothing in my name: ask,
> and ye shall receive, that your joy may be full
> (John 16:23-24).

These verses of Scripture clearly express the differences in
the believer's employment of the Name of Jesus. One (John
14:13-14) talks about establishing a thing, making a demand
or a declaration in the Name of Jesus; the other (John 16:23-

24) talks about making a request to the Father in the Name of Jesus and the Father's obligation to grant your request.

Note: There's a difference between when a thing has to be established and when it has to be given.

When Jesus said, "Whatsoever ye shall ask the Father in my name, he will give it you" (John 16:23), He wasn't referring to us demanding that something be done in His name. But when He said, "If ye shall ask any thing in my name, I will do it" (John 14:14), He was talking about getting something done, establishing or decreeing a thing in His name.

The statement in John 14:13-14 doesn't refer to praying to God the Father, but using the Name of Jesus to deal with situations in our daily lives. Here, Jesus is saying, "When you make a declaration, I'll cause it to happen; I'll back you up!"

When we speak or make declarations in the Name of Jesus, we're taking His place and standing in His stead as Master over all things. This is not the same as using His name to ask things from Him, which is unscriptural.

MAKING DECLARATIONS IN HIS NAME

When we make declarations in the Name of Jesus, circumstances, devils, demons, sicknesses, diseases, and infirmities are obliged to listen and obey. Whether we shout excitedly about it, or we just say it calmly and casually, we've been ordained to get results. Jesus said when you pray, don't be like the heathens, who think they will be heard for their much speaking (Matthew 6:7).

This reminds me of the encounter between Elijah and the prophets of Baal. They called on their god to send down fire, but he wouldn't respond. Then Elijah taunted them, "Come on, cry louder. Maybe Baal went on a journey. He must come back today!" And they went on and on, ranting and raving and calling on Baal to answer them.

The Bible says they even cut themselves until they bled all over, and still Baal didn't respond. But when it was Elijah's turn, he didn't have to repeat himself like the prophets of Baal. He just said, "O God, let these people know You sent me. Send fire from heaven and light up this thing!" God answered, and the fire came down (1 Kings 18:19-40).

Faith came to us when we received the gospel and passed from darkness into the light of the kingdom of God's dear Son. That's why we're not required to have faith to use the Name of Jesus and to do things in His name. We already had that faith when we were born again, according to Romans 12:3: "God hath dealt to every man the measure of faith." We're not trying to beg for something; we're possessors!

The Name of Jesus Christ has been given to us as a blank cheque endorsed with our name on it. You can fill anything in that cheque because your Father's bank is a big one. You want divine health? Then fill it in! You can say, "In the Name of Jesus, I walk in divine health from this day forward. They're not taking me to that hospital again!" That sickness will have to leave when you use the Name of Jesus!

You can make decrees in Jesus' name and have them established unto you. You can ask the Father in the Name of Jesus for whatever you desire and receive it so your joy can be full.

CHAPTER FOUR

THE "REAL" LORD'S PRAYER

In this chapter, we will take some time to critically examine what is commonly referred to as the Lord's Prayer. I made reference to this subject in chapter two, and now I will explain it in detail. We will look at the Lord's Prayer from a purely scriptural viewpoint and clear up many of the misconceptions about it that have been passed down in the Church over the years.

The disciples of Jesus prompted Him to teach them that prayer recorded in Matthew 6, popularly known as the Lord's Prayer. When Jesus taught them this prayer, they were all still under the Old Testament. The New Testament hadn't come into effect because Jesus hadn't yet died.

Here, we'll get to see more reasons why we shouldn't pray this prayer. The Lord Jesus prayed in Matthew 6:9-13:

> Our Father which art in heaven, Hallowed be thy

name. Thy kingdom come. Thy will be done in earth, as it is in heaven. Give us this day our daily bread. And forgive us our debts, as we forgive our debtors. And lead us not into temptation, but deliver us from evil: For thine is the kingdom, and the power, and the glory, for ever. Amen.

This is the Lord's Prayer, and it is recited in almost every school in every nation where they pray to God as Christians and in many homes where they chorus it in a singsong. Everybody loves it; they say it's the Lord's Prayer, but Jesus never called it His prayer.

I want you to understand that Jesus taught on the subject of prayer in a way that's different from what we can practice now. There was the Old Testament way of praying, and now there's the New Testament way of praying. What people call the Lord's Prayer is not for the Christian. You might as well say, "Twinkle, twinkle little star, how I wonder what you are, Amen," and expect the same results as when you pray this prayer.

If you're born again, you don't have any business praying this prayer, and I'll tell you why: We're not living in the Old Testament but in the New Testament. In fact, if you've been praying this prayer, God has not been hearing you. You may not like that, but it's the truth.

You may have felt really spiritual each time you recited it, but that doesn't matter. It's no prayer, and it didn't work. Am I saying this because I don't like this prayer? No. I used to say the same prayer several years ago. I thought it was right, then I found out it was wrong. If we don't find things out from the Word of God, we will never know and will continue to grope in the darkness of ignorance.

Now I'm going to show you some things from the Bible, then you can make up your mind, and you better make up your mind right! But you must realize that you can make the right decision only when you've got the right information.

Don't get sentimental about this. Don't say, "My grandfather prayed this prayer, my father prayed it, and I was raised in a church where we prayed it every day." It doesn't make any difference who taught you to recite this prayer. The important question to ask is, Is it right? Let's answer that question now.

THE LORD'S PRAYER –OR IS IT?

First, the Lord's Prayer as most people know it is not a New Testament prayer at all. There are two prayers by Jesus recorded in the New Testament. I've often said that the New Testament doesn't begin at the book of Matthew like most Bible publishers indicate. The New Testament actually started after the death of Jesus in John 19:30. Nonetheless, the Bible is divided into two sections: Genesis to Malachi, being the Old Testament section, and Matthew to Revelation, being the New Testament section.

The first prayer, which most people refer to as the Lord's

Prayer, was not His prayer at all. This I will prove to you shortly.

The disciples came to Jesus and asked Him, "Master, teach us how to pray as John taught his disciples" (Luke 11:1).

Jesus answered and said, "After this manner pray ye." In other words, "I'll give you a guideline." Then He started, "Our Father which art in heaven, Hallowed be thy name." At that time, this prayer was okay. It said, "Thy kingdom come" because at the time He was teaching them, the kingdom hadn't yet come. But now the kingdom has already come. In the epistles, you'll discover this prayer has been abolished.

We need to find out what to pray about and how to pray from the New Testament. When you say "New Testament," it presupposes that there is an old one. There is a better word for "testament," which is "will." When a man makes a will, it can only come into effect after his death. As long as he's alive, you can't execute it. You'd be wrong to do that.

> For where a testament is, there must also of necessity be the death of the testator. For a testament is of force after men are dead: otherwise it is of no strength at all while the testator liveth (Hebrews 9:16-17).

The New International Version puts it this way:

> In the case of a will, it is necessary to prove the death of the one who made it, because a will is

in force only when somebody has died; it never takes effect while the one who made it is living.

The point is, until a man dies, his will is of no power. In most Bible translations, the publishers indicate the New Testament starting from the book of Matthew, and I say that's not exactly true. In these Bibles, after the book of Malachi, there's a page that reads, "The New Testament of our Lord Jesus Christ," and then the page right next to that starts the Gospel according to Saint Matthew.

The New Testament couldn't have started with the birth of Jesus because there couldn't have been one until He died. This means everything He taught before He died would need to be clearly understood to know if they were applicable only to those in the Old Testament (which was still in effect at the time before His death) or also applicable after His death.

Notice that when He taught them to pray this prayer before His death, His name was never used. In the New Testament, we're commanded to pray in His name. Back then they couldn't have used His name because it didn't yet have the power for salvation.

This is one reason the Lord's Prayer as it is popularly known is not a New Testament prayer. It was taught to the people of the Old Testament. Anyone today who prays: "Our father which art in heaven, Hallowed be thy name. Thy kingdom come . . ." is praying like the Old Testament folks should have prayed, and that wouldn't work today because that contract has ended. We now live in a new contract, under a new agreement, a *will* brought into force by the death of our Lord Jesus Christ.

Jesus Himself said, "In that day you shall not pray to Me, but whatever you shall ask the Father in My name, He will give to you. Until now you haven't asked anything in My name; ask that your joy may be full" (John 16:23-24). "That day" is the day of the new agreement or contract. After His resurrection, we're supposed to pray to the Father in His name.

Now, let's see certain points about this prayer that disqualify it as the Lord's Prayer and why it should not be prayed by the Christian in the New Testament.

> After this manner therefore pray ye: Our Father which art in heaven, Hallowed be thy name. Thy kingdom come. Thy will be done in earth, as it is in heaven (Matthew 6:9-10)

#1. IT'S JUST A PATTERN

In the first place, Jesus was only showing a pattern of prayer because He said, "After this manner therefore pray ye." You ought to understand that Jesus wasn't teaching us to pray this prayer, but showing us a guideline, letting us understand that in prayer, we begin by worshipping and praising God: "Our Father which art in heaven, Hallowed be thy name."

#2. THE KINGDOM HAS COME

At the time Jesus taught His disciples to pray this prayer, the kingdom hadn't yet come. So He prayed, "Thy kingdom come." But we're in His kingdom now. Colossians 1:12-13 says, "Giving thanks unto the Father, which hath made us meet (qualified) to be partakers of the inheritance of the saints in light: Who hath delivered us from the power of darkness, and hath translated us into the kingdom of his dear Son."

Did you notice this is in the past tense? It didn't say He *shall make* us meet, but He *hath made* us meet. He already has qualified us to be partakers of the inheritance of the saints in light. It also says that He "hath delivered us from the power of darkness, and hath translated us into the kingdom of his dear Son."

The word "translated" means "transferred"; that is, "to take from one place to another." We've been taken out of darkness into the kingdom of His dear Son. It doesn't say He shall translate us into the kingdom of His dear Son; He already has done it! We're in His kingdom now. So the prayer "Thy kingdom come" was answered a long time ago.

#3. OUR DAILY BREAD ALREADY HAS BEEN GIVEN

Give us this day our daily bread (Matthew 6:11).

When Adam and Eve listened to the serpent and ate of the

fruit of the tree from which God had forbidden them to eat, they committed high treason against Him and fell from His grace. By that singular act, they transferred their authority over the earth to Satan and brought a curse upon it: "Cursed is the ground for thy sake; in sorrow shalt thou eat of it all the days of thy life; thorns also and thistles shall it bring forth to thee; and thou shalt eat the herb of the field; in the sweat of thy face shalt thou eat bread, till thou return unto the ground; for out of it wast thou taken: for dust thou art, and unto dust shalt thou return" (Genesis 3:17-19).

The devil had assumed man's authority over the earth, and for man's needs to be met, he had to call upon God's higher authority to prevail against the devil. This is why in the Old Testament, they had to pray to God for such blessings.

But thanks be to God, Jesus has broken the devil's hold over the earth! He stripped the devil of all his power and authority (Colossians 2:15) and gave to us the same authority He has over all things, including the earth and the devil himself (Matthew 28:18-20). Now, we don't need to ask God, "Give us this day our daily bread"; we can bless the earth and command it to bring forth its increase.

That's why Paul says in 1 Corinthians 3:21-23, "Therefore let no man glory in men for all things are yours; whether Paul, or Apollos, or Cephas, or the world, or life, or death, or things present, or things to come; all are yours; and ye are Christ's; and Christ is God's."

David said, "The earth is the Lord's, and the fulness thereof; the world, and they that dwell therein" (Psalm 24:1).

But now we own it all together with Him. So now we don't pray, "Father, give us our daily bread," or, "Give me a house," "Give me a car," or, "Lord, I need new clothes . . ." Don't pray like that anymore because you have arrived in the kingdom – the land of plenty. You've been brought into a large place, and all things are yours now. Glory to God!

#4. DEBTS ALREADY HAVE BEEN FORGIVEN

> And forgive us our debts, as we forgive our debtors (Matthew 6:12).

This is once again a wrong prayer. You'll discover what's wrong with this as we read further:

> For if ye forgive men their trespasses, your heavenly Father will also forgive you: But if ye forgive not men their trespasses, neither will your Father forgive your trespasses (Matthew 6:14-15).

This makes God's forgiveness of your sins pre-conditioned on your forgiving others, and that really isn't consistent with New Testament doctrine. God didn't forgive us because we forgave others. It's so important you understand this point because the devil has used it to destroy a lot of lives. Old Testament Law said, "An eye for an eye; a tooth for a tooth.

Do to others what you want them to do to you." So if you wanted God to forgive you, you had to forgive others first; thus your forgiveness was pre-conditioned on your forgiving others.

But it isn't so. You're not forgiven because you forgave someone else; you're not blessed because you blessed someone else. Forgiveness is your inheritance. You're forgiven because it's part of the package in the new contract. And you don't just forgive because you want your heavenly Father to forgive you; you forgive because you're born after Him; you have His nature. Your Father forgives, and since you're like Him, you necessarily forgive.

God is our example. The Bible says, "And be ye kind one to another, tenderhearted, forgiving one another, even as God for Christ's sake hath forgiven you" (Ephesians 4:32). So we forgive because we love to; we forgive because our heavenly Father forgives and we're like Him. Thus in the New Testament, we're not given a law to forgive first before we are forgiven. This is why we can't pray this prayer in Matthew 6:12, because it makes forgiveness pre-conditioned on something we have to do. And in the New Testament, there's no blessing that is pre-conditioned on anything but on the shed blood of Jesus Christ. Hallelujah!

#5. WE ALREADY ARE DELIVERED

And lead us not into temptation, but deliver us

from evil (Matthew 6:13).

The word "evil" here is from a Greek noun "poneros," which means "the evil one." Some translations, such as the Amplified Bible and the New International Version, read, "deliver us from the evil one." Here the Lord was talking about the one who's responsible for evil, not necessarily an evil act, and we know who that is – the devil.

If we pray "deliver us from evil," then it means we're still subject to the devil. We can't accept that because He already told us in Colossians 1:13 that we've been delivered from the power and domain of darkness. They prayed this prayer then because at that time, the evil one still had power over them and God was their succour. So they had to pray to Him to deliver them from the evil one. But now He says, "these signs shall follow them that believe; in my name shall they cast out devils" (Mark 16:17). To be able to cast out devils surely means you have authority over them. Praise God!

In the New Testament, after the resurrection of the Lord Jesus Christ, there is no place in the Bible that suggests we should pray about the devil or ask God's help against him.

When Jesus came out of the grave, He said, "All power (that is, authority) is given unto me in heaven and in earth. Go ye therefore" (Matthew 28:18-19). What this means is, "I've got all the power and authority; now go in My name, in My power, and in My authority!"

This is not a promise. Moreover, the Father has declared that at the Name of Jesus every knee should bow (Philippians

2:10). So all the devils are aware; they know they've got to bow at the Name of Jesus because it's the name above every name. Hallelujah!

We're not going to be delivered from evil because we've already been delivered from evil, and all the devils and evil powers have been placed under our feet. What we're required to do is use the Name of Jesus to keep them there. Therefore, this prayer, "deliver us from evil," is not consistent with New Testament doctrine.

There's a new kind of prayer for the New Testament. This Lord's Prayer was not for the New Testament; it was not prayed in Jesus' name, for the use of His name had not been revealed. He hadn't been given all power and authority, and you could only exercise authority in His name to a certain limit. But when He died and was buried and rose again, He said, "Go into all the world and make disciples of all nations in My name." Now He calls us His living proof producers, not only in Jerusalem, Judea, and Samaria, but in the uttermost parts of the earth (Acts 1:8). Praise God!

The "Real" Lord's Prayer

From the many proofs I've shown you from the Scriptures, it's apparent that "the Lord's Prayer" is really not "Our Father which art in heaven . . .," found in Matthew 6. However, there's a prayer of the Lord Jesus in Saint John's Gospel, chapter 17. That's really the "Lord's prayer" because it's a kingdom prayer, as we shall see:

> These words spake Jesus, and lifted up his eyes
> to heaven, and said, Father, the hour is come;
> glorify thy Son, that thy Son also may glorify
> thee: As thou hast given him power over all
> flesh, that he should give eternal life to as many
> as thou hast given him. And this is life eternal,
> that they might know thee the only true God,
> and Jesus Christ, whom thou hast sent. I have
> glorified thee on the earth: I have finished the
> work which thou gavest me to do. And now, O
> Father, glorify thou me with thine own self with
> the glory which I had with thee before the world
> was (John 17:1-5).

This is a beautiful prayer Jesus prayed in line with what He had taught His disciples. Notice that His prayer of praise at the beginning is a confession, not of sins, but of God's works in His life. He said, "Father, the hour has come. Glorify Me, that I also may glorify You. You have given Me power over all flesh, that I should give eternal life to as many as You have given Me."

In just the same way, you should declare, "Father, I worship You today. Let Your name be glorified in me that I also may glorify You, as You have given me authority to function in the Name of Jesus."

Jesus knew Who He was, and He said it; He confessed it in

His prayers. He said, "You (Father) have given Me power over all flesh . . ." This is "the Lord's prayer" for real!

It's good to know what's in the Book. God said, "My people are destroyed (they suffer and perish) for lack of knowledge" (Hosea 4:6). It's not a lack of the knowledge of physics, chemistry, architecture, or medicine, but knowledge of the Word of God. But thank God, we're finding out; the Word is building our faith strong, and we're developing in the things of the Spirit. We're becoming more knowledgeable in prayer.

my people perish for a lack of knowledge ? of the word !

CHAPTER FIVE

A MODEL PRAYER

Now that you've learned the right approach to prayer in the New Testament, put the things you've learned to work immediately. Start practicing the right kind of prayer, and do away with the wrong mind-sets, perceptions, practices, and prayers that have made your prayer life ineffective.

Below is a prayer of the Spirit based on God's Word that will help you get started on the right path:

Dear Father, in the Name of the Lord Jesus, I thank You for Your Word that has come to me through this book. I receive it into my spirit with meekness, gladness and faith. Your Word is mixed with faith in my heart, and I am energized from within by the Holy Spirit to put it to work. I declare that as I put Your Word to work in my prayer life, it produces the right results; my profiting through Your Word becomes evident as I receive answers to my prayers, in Jesus' name.

Thank You, Lord, for blessing me so much. I'm blessed in my spirit, my soul, and my body. I'm blessed in my going out and in my coming in. Everything I lay my hands upon to do prospers in the Name of Jesus. Thank You for Your wisdom that You've made available to me. The wisdom of God is functioning in me, causing me to think right, speak right, and act right. I'm walking in the blessing and in the glory of God, in the mighty Name of Jesus Christ. Amen.

This is a good place to start, but remember, it's just a start. As you delve into the Word, especially the New Testament epistles of Paul the apostle, you'll discover many more prayer points that will greatly increase your knowledge and vocabulary in prayer, and, in turn, enrich your prayer life.

Now you can enjoy an increasingly joyous, glorious, victorious, and prosperous life in the Lord as you pray the right way and receive answers to your prayers.

LoveWorld Publications & Tapes Ministry...

Audio & Video Tapes
Audio & Video Cds
Books
Devotionals

Reaching out with the gospel, Building up the saints,
With excellence and clarity.

'Join This Chariot' is a classic on soul winning that motivates the believer to effective evangelism and teaches him practical steps to reaching his world with the gospel of Jesus Christ.
In this book, Pastor Chris teaches divine truths about 'chariots' as God's tools for soul winning. He reveals that God's call to Philip to "... join... this chariot" (Acts 8: 29) is to every believer in every generation, challenges you to answer that call and shows you how to maximize your chariot for world evan-gelization.

Newly Revised Edition

Each chapter ends with an activity sheet designed to aid personal evangelism

Printed in the USA
CPSIA information can be obtained
at www.ICGtesting.com
LVHW041924160624
783316LV00002B/267

9 781597 813334